T0123468

No Time for Poverty

Poverty

JOANN LAMBERT
and
LILA WESLEY

InspiringVoices®

A Service of **Guideposts**

Inspiring Voices books may be ordered through booksellers or by contacting:

Inspiring Voices
1663 Liberty Drive
Bloomington, IN 47403
www.inspiringvoices.com
1-(866) 697-5313

ISBN: 978-1-4624-0651-7 (sc)
ISBN: 978-1-4624-0652-4 (e)

Library of Congress Control Number: 2013909478

Printed in the United States of America.

Inspiring Voices rev. date: 06/13/2013

Contents

Mom Told Me So...

Mom started this book by writing a letter to her grandchildren. In this letter she tells them about growing up during the depression. Her main purpose was to encourage them to have faith during hard times. She would write until her hand cramped, then we would finish by her dictating to me She wrote things down as she remembered them. I then arranged them into chapters. The chapters contain subject matter rather than a time frame.

I treasure the memory of the two of us working together to express the blessings the Lord had bestowed on us. We laughed sometimes, cried sometimes, as we reminisced. We lived together a total of 54 years, but I never felt close to her until we wrote this book.

Eighteen months later we sent it to a publisher. Mom was excited about seeing our work in a book form. However, she died on January 26, 2013 without seeing her wish come true.

Here it is Mom your life story in print.

JoAnn

CHAPTER 1

Missouri

As I sit here in my breakfast room, on this cold dreary day January 17, 2011. I am thinking about some of the questions my grand-kids and great grand-kids asked me at our Christmas get together. I am writing this down to tell them about growing up in a small Indiana town during the 1920's and 1930's. The tree is down and all the decorations put away for another year. I have plenty of time to write and reminisce.

Today is Martin Luther King Jr. day. Now a national holiday, it is also my 95th birthday. Almost everything is closed. No mail or banking. I feel honored. The bird feeders outside the window are really crowded with cardinals, blue jays and one redheaded woodpecker. Doves and squirrels come to visit also. We need to thank God for them. They are parts of our lives given to us for enjoyment.

Now, back to my life story, I was born in Gideon, Missouri Jan 17, 1916 to Isaac and Caroline [Jaynes] Deckard. My dad answered to the name of Ike and mother was Carrie. I was named after my grandma Deckard, Delila Jayne. I answer to Lila. When I was born mother was ill with yellow jaundice. I weighed three pounds and two ounces. She couldn't breast feed me, however, she told me about an angel God sent to us. An old man named Scottie Lewis lived behind us and he had a goat. He milked that goat every two hours and fed me. He carried me on a pillow, even changed my diapers. He had to be an angel. Now you know why I am so stubborn, it was the goat milk. Scottie died when I was about two years old. Mother told me that I would watch for him and cry. To this day I can see him taking care of children in Heaven.

I remember little about living in Missouri. When I was three years old, dad and mother went to the grocery store leaving Edith the oldest, age 9 to care for us. Oma age 7 and Grant was 5 years old. Just kids. Edith told mother that Grant got mad at me and held my right hand next to a hot belly stove [our heater] I still have the scar yet today. All mother said was boys will be boys.

World War I was going on. Dad worked for the railroad as an engineer and also part time at the mill in Gideon. Four children and mother expecting kept dad from going to war. Odes was born in 1918. He lived to be eighteen months. He died with pneumonia. A lot of people died around that time. Mother said the flu was really bad and there weren't many doctors back then. Another sadness, Tommy was an early birth born in 1919, mother had the flu and the baby lived just a few hours. I can remember riding in the wagon taking him to the cemetery.

I also remember we lived in a two story house with a big front porch. Dad made a porch swing but Edith and Oma told me I was too little for the swing so I couldn't sit in it. Dad made a little swing just for me, I was so happy with it mother said she had a hard time getting me to do anything but swing. One Christmas dad came home with me a rocking horse. Edith and Oma each a chair and Grant a wagon. He used scrap lumber but painted them pretty. It was a good Christmas. I don't think I will ever forget how proud we were.

Mother rented two rooms upstairs to two men. Daniel worked at the mill, he was a young man. John was older, just got out of the army. He lost his left leg and left eye. A really nice man, he told us stories and read to us. Mother cooked for them. Daniel was a big guy and ate a lot. Mother told us he had a girlfriend and he was gone most of the time.

July 1920, Gail came into our lives he was the prettiest little baby. I was four then and wanted to take care of him. I couldn't remember Odes you just forget at that age.

1 Peter 1:3
His divine power has given us everything we need
for life and godliness through our knowledge of Him
who called us by His glory and goodness.

CHAPTER 2

The Move To Indiana

IN THE SPRING of 1922 Dad wanted to move back to Indiana. His brother Charley was moving back. He came earlier to visit Grandpa Deckard who wasn't very well. Uncle Charley bought a farm down by the locks on the Wabash River. It was a really nice house with outbuildings. It even had a bathroom with water in the house. He returned to Missouri to move his family to the Hoosier state. He talked my Dad into moving back also. Mother didn't want to leave her family and she didn't want Dad to quit his job. What else could she do, five kids and another one on the way she didn't have much choice. The move wasn't so good for Mother. We spent our first night on this side of the Mississippi River in Illinois at a sleazy boarding house. Bedbugs were really bad, none of us slept much. Next morning after breakfast it was train time again; next stop was St. Francisville, Illinois. There we changed trains again in the middle of the night. For extra money a man brought us into Indiana, to a farm next to Brevort elevator. Another brother, Uncle Bill lived across the road. Three of Uncle Bill's kids, two of Uncle Charley's and five of us slept on the floor. Ten kids sleeping on the living room floor was fun laughing and talking.

Esco and I were six years old. Gail was two and the others were older and smarter or so they thought.

Next morning Uncle Bill took us down to Beal a little stop in the road about ten miles south of Vincennes and across the river from St Francisville. Beal consisted of a Methodist church, a one room school, a dirty grocery store and a blacksmith shop run by Uncle Len, another brother.

Grandpa and Grandma lived in a two story house. We all stayed with them until our belongings arrived. Then Uncle Charley and Aunt Meg left to move in their house. Dad couldn't find a house for us. Everett, a cousin to me but Dad's age, son of his older sister found us a house that had been moved out of the flood water. It was bad with no floors. Thank God it was spring. Grandpa died and we moved in with Grandma. Vivian was born July 27, 1922.

School started, I wanted to go, and I was six in January. Mother said I was too little. I was big enough to wash diapers and potty train Gail. It didn't take to long for that job to get old. Gail was a good kid and we become great buddies.

Reverend Chessy, who lived in St. Francisville, wanted to have a revival. But there was no place to have a meeting. Uncle Len told him he could use the blacksmith shop. The revival sure did wake up the people. First time they ever heard of the Pentecostal faith. Rev. Chessy preached against bobbed hair, jewelry and women's short sleeve clothing. The women started wearing long dresses with long sleeves, no makeup, etc. The men gave up smoking, drinking home brew, etc.

The church grew. They built the church that still stands today. The ground was given to them by a man Uncle Bill worked for. All the lumber was bought by the men and labor was free. It didn't take long for the men to build the church. It had hardwood pews, heating stove, wood box, pump organ, a podium and hymnbooks. Any kid that wanted to could drive a nail on the outside. That was a big thing for us, about twenty or twenty five kids drove their nail into the building.

A few years ago was the church's eightieth anniversary. Larry, my son, was here visiting and we went to the celebration. It was a great day. Most of the older folks are gone, but the church is still about the same.

Now, there is an oil furnace and two inside restrooms. It's good to go back sometimes. It's only ten miles away from home. Now the building has two restrooms inside, before it had two out houses one for the men and one for the women. An old fashioned heating stove stood in the center of the church…Uncle Tom had a saw-mill where Dad worked and wood was donated to the church. Sometimes someone would buy a load of coal. Edith and I cleaned the church filled the wood box, and cleaned out ashes. We called it paying our tithes.

Mrs. Kolehouse, a very sweet lady who always wore black, would dance around all over the building but never touch the stove. A lot of people shouted, but I never saw my Dad or Mother shout. Uncle Bill became the preacher, Dad the song leader and Uncle John evangelized.

The Christmas before my ninth birthday Uncle Bill invited a preacher from Vincennes to hold a revival for two weeks. Mrs. Kolehouse asks me to keep the wood box filled and clean the church and she would pay me. Since we lived behind the church, I jumped at the chance. She paid me fifty cents, I was so proud of that coin. I must have spent it a dozen times in my head. Finally I gave it to Mother to buy me a doll. I did not remember of ever having a doll. She and Dad went to Vincennes on Saturday and she got me the prettiest eleven inch doll. I loved her so much that I would hardly ever put her down. Christmas day came and a family from across the way came for dinner. Mother wasn't happy about it. She wanted to be a good Christian. The daughter, Mary Ellen took a liking to my doll and wouldn't give it back to me. She then threw one of her little fits. Dad gave it to her, saying he would buy me another one, but he never did. Anyway the brat would say at school "I got Lila's doll". How I hated that girl. I didn't talk to my Dad for a long time. I wondered what I had done for him to dislike me so much. I was a kid also and I had worked for it. I guess some of the goat milk was still in my body, stubborn.

Ruth was born January 6, 1926. There wasn't much going on until spring, planting garden, canning and taking care of Ruth. Loren was 2 years old, Vivian was 4 and Gail was 6. You can see that was a busy time.

In August Dad got a job at the canning factory in St. Francisville so we moved over there. Mother, Edith and Oma went to work at the canning factory also. I was 10 years old. There were four younger kids left in my care. I fixed Ruth sugar titties. Cheese cloth square, sugar butter and dip it in milk. Sound good? She liked them. When the canning season was over, Dad found a few odd jobs, that winter was hard on my family.

My dad wanted to be baptized. For some reason he insisted on being baptized right then and there. It was a hard winter and the river was frozen solid. The men cut a hole in the ice and dad was baptized. How us kids yelled and cried in fear of our daddy getting sick and dying. He never had any harsh side effects, not even a cold.

Acts 20:28
Keep watch over yourselves and all the flock of which the
Holy Spirit has made you overseers. Be shepherds of the
church of God which He bought with His own blood.

CHAPTER 3

Wabash River Flood

IN THE SPRING Uncle Charley needed someone to work on the levee and locks. He rented us a two room house, it wasn't much in fact it was a terrible place. The water came up to the door when the river flooded. We had a boat to get out of the house. If anyone needed to go to town, they had to walk on top of the levee. Mother had a lot of faith or confidence in me. I would put the kids and a mother hen and her seven babies in a boat and go over to the levee to play. We had fun playing with the little chicks. We named them but couldn't tell them apart afterword. We lay on a blanket and played button, button who has the button. I told them stories and played tag. The best part was the kids were good and minded me. I put a pitch fork in the boat to gig fish for supper. The fish would come up and cross the road. I got pretty good gigging fish and frogs. We ate a lot of fish that June. Fresh greens grew on the levee banks. Edith was working in a home for an elderly couple. Oma got married in May after her sixteenth birthday in April. She worked at the cigar factory in Vincennes at the time. This left me the oldest girl to help at home. I was eleven in January. I was always skinny and too small for my age.

After the water went down, Mother and Dad went grocery shopping. They took Grant with them in case they had trouble. They left me home with four kids. Our house was still damp and cold. We had to keep a fire going in the cook stove. I felt old being in charge. My parents trusted me. However, if one of us had to go to the outhouse, we all went.

Our closest neighbors were about one mile away. We had oil lamps, no phone, and no way to get help if we needed it. I must have been pretty brave, I didn't cry or sleep until Mother and Dad got home around midnight.

That summer was really hot. We didn't have any trees or fans. We never dreamed of air conditioning, Me, Gail, Vivian, Loren and sometimes Ruth went over across the levee where there were trees. We threw rocks in the river and picked up mussel shells.

1 Timothy 6:7&8
For we brought nothing into this world and we can take nothing out of it. But if we have food and clothing we will be content with that.

Chapter 4

An Angel Visits

Somehow, we survived the summer of 1927. Paul was born October 9, 1927. Mother had a lot of trouble, but never complained too much. She wasn't well. She had an infection. The doctor said it was caused from not passing all the afterbirth. Abscesses under her arms were so bad she couldn't put her arms down. So again she couldn't breastfeed the baby, Paul. I fed him oatmeal, mashed potatoes, gravy and of course sugar titties. No bottles, we didn't really know what they looked like.

I hated school. It was so far to walk to catch the bus. Snow, rain, and mud were every day hazards. We lined the bottom of our shoes with cardboard or folded paper, whatever we could find. Then to keep our feet from freezing we wrapped them in burlap bags. It was an awful winter for all of us. Dad didn't get much work. Uncle Tom gave him work at his sawmill when the weather was good.

In the spring of 1928 Dad got a job with a gravel company running the engine for $25.00 a week. Times were bad then, but it got worse in later years. Dad rented a two bedroom house for six dollars a month. It had a big yard, garden, rose bushes, lilac bush, chicken house, cellar, smoke house and front and back porches. Dad and Grant spaded up a part of the garden area and planted potatoes, beans, corn and tomatoes. Mother telling them how to do it, she was four feet six or seven inches tall, but she was strong in faith and spirit, she could get things done.

Gail and I had just finished working in the garden, Mother and the kids laid down for a nap. We went to the pump to wash up and to pump water until it was really cold for a drink. We saw a woman coming down the road carrying a suitcase. We didn't see many people on this gravel road. She came up our lane and asks if she could have a drink of our cold water. Gail went inside to get her a glass, she told me her name was Molly. I asked her if she had a family (being a little nosy) she said she wasn't going anywhere in particular. We chatted for a while, and then Mother came outside. Molly jumped up and said "Let us have a prayer for your mother". Then she told me to go get some baking soda, and she took a bottle out of her suitcase made a salve and put on mother. Anyway we helped her fix supper and feed Paul. She said she was going to stay with us until mother got well which was about two weeks. She helped with everything, laundry, scrubbing etc. She slept with me and Paul. I woke up one morning and went to the kitchen. Dad was drinking coffee, I asked him where was Molly. He said she left some time in the night. We never saw or heard from her. I will always believe she was an angel to help us when we needed her the most. She could sing like an angel and she would pray for all of us. I love you Molly where ever you are.

Hebrew 13:1 &2
Keep on loving each other as brothers. Do not forget
to entertain strangers for by so doing some people
have entertained angels without knowing it.

CHAPTER 5

Our Fathers Death

WE WERE DOING so well or so we thought. I was looking forward to school starting. Mother was making Vivian and me new dresses, slips, skirts and blouses. She had put shirts and overalls in the lay a way at J.C. Penny's for Grant and Gail.

Around the middle of August Dad came home from work sick. He didn't feel like getting out of bed. Mother stayed with him most of the time and again I had the kids to look after. After a few days he was feeling a little better. Mother was so tired she laid down to rest on the couch. I took the kids in my bedroom to rest. Later Mother called me for help. Dad was trying to go outside without any clothes on. We had a hard time getting him back to bed. He kept fighting us. I ran down the road to get Mr. Hawkins to come and help us. Then a Mr. Lucas came up and stayed all night. The next morning Dad passed away. His fever was so high, he couldn't fight it anymore. Dr. Snyder came over from St. Francisville and gave us typhoid shots. Which brought back memories of a diphtheria shot we all had when Vivian was diagnosed with it? A contagious disease, we were all quarantined. We missed a half year of school or at least a couple months. I was twelve years old I hated that shot. It hurt.

I tried my best to care for the kids; Mother had so much on her mind. She was left with eight kids. No money, no insurance. My uncle and aunts took over the main part of everything. I was told later God sends His angels to care for us. Mr. and Mrs. Klein who owned the house came and told mother not to worry. We could live there rent free until we were all older or as long as she wanted. You don't find many people like them today. I am looking forward to meeting them in heaven to hug them and say thanks. We love you.

There were a lot of good people. But times were hard for example the article that was printed in our local newspaper not long ago. I want to share it with you kids. The article was written by Brian Spangle. I remember the time he is referring to. People heard about our situation. They were all angels on earth. We found bushels of peaches, canning jars and lids, vegetables, feed sacks, clothes etc. on the porch all times of the day. Some people didn't leave notes to this day all we can say is "Thank you, God bless".

The next six years we lived there was just about the same as everyone else. Depression was bad, no jobs, men worked for $1.50 or $2.00 dollars a day or less just to feed their families. Gail and I walked over the country side doing odd jobs such as cleaning chicken houses, barns, helping in gardens, yards earning 25 or 50 cents a job. Each spring we worked in the tomato field pulling plants. These fields were out Sixth Street Road. Hard work but lots of fun for this we got paid $2.00 a day sun up to sun down. I was fourteen; Gail was ten he could count to 50 so Mr. Gilliat gave him a job. Edith worked also. The job was you pulled 50 plants, laid them behind you in the row and men picked them up to ship out. We picked green beans, tomatoes, and gleaned corn. We saved the best ears to sell to buy clothes, coats, and shoes. Whichever kid needed them the worst got the new things.

Back to the peaches, someone left us three bushels. Mother and I were up all night canning and washing jars. My feet were so swollen I could hardly walk. Mother told me to go soak them for a while and lay down. After I rested it was her turn and I cleaned up the mess and fed the kids.

Those peach cobblers sure tasted good that winter. Coming home from school Mother had one in the oven. We must have canned at least seven or eight bushels that summer. She also canned green beans, peas, and corn she also made vegetable soup from everything left in the garden. She buried the potatoes, carrots and turnips. She made sauerkraut, nothing was wasted. Sauerkraut dumplings tasted real good on a winter day, the core or the heart of the cabbage was creamed German style and canned. What a treat on a cold day.

Spring of 1929, school was out and our work began. Planting garden again, people were good to us by giving us seeds and plants, plowing our garden. Yet today I miss the garden work, seeing things grow is a miracle. Like a new born baby's first smile, crawling, walking and talking. Next thing before you realize it they are changing into grownups. I wondered some times where I am in this cycle of human life.

After Labor Day we started school at Consolidated #2 or some people called it Bunker Hill. It was first grade thru eighth grade. Grant, Gail, Vivian and I were in school. This left three still at home, Paul, Ruth and Loren. I don't know how mother did all the things she did washing clothes on the washboard, ironing, cooking and taking care of all of us. She never complained. We kids all had chores to do. Feed the chickens, fill wood boxes and bring in enough water for the next day.

Romans 12:13-16
Share with God's people who are in need. Practice
hospitality. Bless those who persecute you, bless and do not
curse. Rejoice with those who rejoice; mourn with those
who mourn. Live in harmony with one another.

Chapter 6

Mean People

THERE ARE GOOD and bad in each of us. I know mother hated to apply for welfare and put up with some of the remarks people made, like our caseworker, Mrs. E we called her. Mother was supposed to receive $12 a week, Mrs. E. gave her $3 and she kept the $9. She told Mother since we lived in the country and grew lots of our food, raised chickens and did washings and ironing for people that $3 a week was all she could get. Mrs. E. bought a new model A Ford. She told us kids not to touch the car; she didn't want finger prints on her pretty new car. How can people be like that? One day Mrs. Klein came to the house and the welfare money was mentioned in the conversation. Of course big mouth me; I had to tell Mrs. Klein how much Mother received. She said we should get more. She went to the welfare office and discovered what was going on. I don't know what happened to Mrs. E, but she had to pay Mother all the money she had stolen. There were other families that were involved too.

Mother bought margarine in a carton that had a small package of coloring to mix in it to look like butter. It tasted good too. Mrs. E. came in one day when I was mixing the oleo. She asks me what it cost, I didn't know. She said "Don't buy that anymore, use lard on your bread it's cheaper". That's when I had it with her and asked "Is that what you feed your fat son?" she left in an angry mood. Every now and then I can hear my mother say "Watch your temper Lila".

There is one thing I cannot tolerate is someone being mean to other people. There was a boy that rode the school bus, he was a big bully. He thought everyone was afraid of him. He would get on the bus first, and lay down on the seat. A lot of us had to stand up it was a long ride for many of the little kids. We were the third stop. The kids would yell Klein station, Lane station, and Deckard station, all in fun. Mr. Henry the driver was an older man, I think he was afraid of Ray the bully. But I wasn't. One day I thought this is enough, so I asked Ray to sit up and let the kids sit down. When he didn't budge, I grabbed him by the feet and pulled him off the bus. I convinced him that he would be better off sitting up. After that Ray sat up behind Mr. Henry. I don't remember him ever speaking to me again.

Another incident I remember was lunch time at school and we were all outside. It came up a cold rain and sleet. Mrs. Dehl the principal came in the room and stated there was some that just don't obey the rules. When the bell rings they better come in. She looked at me and said that means your sister also. I got up and left so did several others. She had locked the doors and the kids could not get inside. Along with my sister Vivian was Mary Sue's sister Grace, Hugh's sister Ethel Mae, Bernard's sister Mildred and Ada's sister Helen. We went straight to the furnace room for Mr. Joyce. We asked him to open the door. Mrs. Dehl was right behind us, she gave the OK. I told her "If my sister gets sick, Mother will send you the doctor bill". The parents had a meeting and Mrs. Dehl got fired. She could be real nice but she liked to be in control of everything. She let her job go to her head like a lot of people do.

We thought Betsy our cow was being mean by getting out of her pen and getting in the neighbor's field. This neighbor held Betsy hostage until dad paid him $5.00. This happened several times until dad built a pen closer to the house and better. The neighbor had three girls about my age and a son older. The kids would laugh about my dad paying to get Betsy back.

Years later I was working in a store downtown when the youngest girl came in. After we visited for a while she brought up the subject of our cow. She told me her dad made her brother let our cow out of her pen and put her in their field. He needed the $5.00 to get supplies for his still. She also said her mother got mad at him, but was afraid of him. He was a very mean man to his family and everyone else too. I pray that God gave him some mercy.

Another neighbor Mr. C came to the house and got angry with Mother. He said us kids were stealing his corn. Mother told him we had a larger plot of sweet corn. Why would we steal his field corn? She said we would watch and see who is stealing the corn. We found out it was the bootleggers kids. He used it to make corn whiskey.

I was working in a large department store, the largest in our town. One of our coworkers didn't like to wait on people with mental problems. We had one customer that had cerebral palsy and was hard to understand. She went to school with JoAnn. She knew me and would wait for me to help her. The coworker would stand behind her and mock her. I told her "you shouldn't do that, sometimes what goes around comes around." She had a beautiful daughter who was attending the University. On the daughter's way home one day a drunken driver hit her head on. She was hurt pretty bad and had brain damage. Her life was all messed up. She married but it didn't last. She ended up committing suicide. The coworker came to see me one day and said she would never forget what I told her when we worked together. Then she started crying. She asks to have prayer with her. She is now deceased.

I have been blessed with good friends and neighbors I can trust. They are there for me if I need them. I have met a lot of people who are so mean and selfish toward other people, all I can do is pray for them. If you ever run into someone like that pray for them that they will change. We can see a lot of that in the last few years from our leaders. Pray for them also.

Country kids got out of school in April. It was my last year at Number Two School. I wanted to go to High school so bad. Mrs. E. said I should get a job instead and help my mother.

Uncle Charley and Aunt Maggie told me if I would help them that summer they would send me to school (Decker Chapel). I was so excited about going that I believed them. So my summer was a big joke, I worked my butt off. I worked from day light till after dark planting garden, feeding baby chickens. Uncle Charley had about four to six hired hands. I did a lot of cooking, dish washing, laundry, ironing and canning etc. When school started they changed their minds. They couldn't afford books and clothes. Not even a thank you or dime of pay.

I went back home to help Mother with her laundry jobs. No piece of clothing ever left without being checked for ripped seams, missing buttons or a patch if needed. We used homemade lye soap, boiling kettle and bluing in the rinse water. A lot of scrubbing and a lot of love went into those baskets. Sometimes a Bible verse or a saying out of a book was tucked in with the clothes. In the spring a bunch of radishes, onions, leaf lettuce etc. Anything that couldn't be canned was given away instead of letting it go to waste.

Romans 12:19-21
Do not take revenge my friends but leave room for God's wrath, for it is written: "It is mine to avenge; I will repay" says the Lord. On the contrary: "If your enemy is hungry, feed him if he is thirsty, give him something to drink. In doing this, you will heap burning coals on his head. Do not be overcome by evil, but overcome evil with good.

CHAPTER 7

My Childhood

COLD AND RAINY days we played school taking turns being the teacher. We all learned a lot in this game. Paper dolls were popular with Vivian, Ruth and me. We cut them out of the old Sears catalog. The boys didn't like this game very much. They played checkers and tic-tac-toe. Loren didn't like to lose so he quit before the game was over, being a big baby. We have a lot of them today, don't you be one. Snow days were fun we wrapped up warm and went down the hill on our home made sled. We made snowmen and had snow ball fights and end up eating snow ice cream. Don't forget our chores came first, we were all Mother had to help after Dad was gone.

Summer time was great we played baseball London Bridge is falling down, jumped rope, and swung on the tire swing. We played tag, kick the can and made up games as we thought them up. Sunday afternoons were really special, all the kids from around would gather at our house to play baseball and some the games listed above. We all enjoyed walking the rails to see who could stay on the longest time. There was no train on Sunday so the grain elevator was closed. Mother was pretty strict about us going anywhere, she wanted to know what was going on and that we didn't get in trouble. She really loved us. She played games with us sometimes, although she kept busy with her work. Some Sundays there would be as many as fifteen or twenty kids in our yard and front porch. Little kids played jacks or with dolls. Older kids played baseball. I love baseball yet today.

I know she missed Dad, left a widow at thirty six years old with eight kids at home. One night I heard her crying. I got up to see about her, she was really upset. I laid down beside her and cried with her for a while. Put my arms around her and promised her "Mother we will make it we have each other and we have God to help us. We won't be kids forever; we will grow up and work. Remember what Dad always said "Just pray about it and some way or another God will provide.

I never saw mother mad until one Saturday she went to town. It was close to Christmas. The kids ask about a tree. Across the railroad were quite a few pine trees. We decided to go cut a limb off and decorate it. The tree was pretty. We made paper chains of dolls. One for girls and one for boys the kids colored them. We were all so proud of our creation. The first Christmas tree we ever had. Mother came home she grabbed that tree stomped on it and started yelling. "You kids trying to send me to hell?" I ask her what she was talking about. She got the Bible and read Jeremiah chapter 10 and verses 2 thru 5. Read this passage and judge for yourself.

Dad was a good hearted man, sometimes too good. We kids knew if the weather was fair on Sunday a family from southern Illinois would come over for church. A man his wife and their four children. Dad would invite them to our house for dinner. Mother would fry at least three chickens, have vegetables from the garden, and bake pies or cobblers. As guest they got to eat first. We had to wait. They ate like it was the last day of their lives. If anything was left I remember the dad telling his kids they better eat more as they wouldn't have supper till late. They would leave early to attend their church for night services.

Mother would fry more chicken and cook vegetables for us kids after they left. I told dad and mother it wasn't right that we had to wait. If I ever had children I would fix their plates first then the guest could eat what was left. That has been my policy for my children and grandchildren to this day.

Don't think playing games was all that went on at Deckard station. We all had chores to do. Early morning and late evening gardening was done. No weeds grew in mother's gardens. I remember how proud she was of her garden; she sure had a green thumb.

About a mile south of us was a blackberry patch. So guess what? The spring of 1929 mother, Edith, Gail and I took a #2 wash tub and smaller pails to put the berries in as we picked them. The berries were so big and sweet we didn't want to miss any. We took turns carrying the tub full of berries home. Then we spent the afternoon canning and eating the sweet berries. It was fun and also a lot of hard work. Edith got poison ivy, so that ended her berry picking days. Oma came and sit with the kids. Mother made her a cobbler to take home with her for their supper.

There was also sadness. Across the road and the railroad was a gravel pit with clear water. A lot of people from town came out there to swim. We would wade around the edge. We were not allowed to get in very far, just paddle our feet mostly. One day we were working in the yard we saw this car go across the railroad a black couple a boy about eight or nine years old, and a couple of other people. If I remember it was two other women.

All of a sudden we heard loud voices calling for someone. The little boy came running toward us. He wanted us to call for help. We didn't have a phone, mother told me to run up to Klein's and have someone call the sheriff's department to come out. I was so out of breath I couldn't talk. Bertie Klein was home, in a wheel chair, he had me write down what was going on. He called the sheriff for me. God bless him. You know me I ran home not wanting to miss anything. The sheriff was there in quick time. He brought a young man with him that was a diver. The diver went down in this hole and brought her up after several tries. I guess she was caught on a rock or limb, we never found out for sure. After that there wasn't much going on at the gravel pit hole. I felt so sorry for the little boy that I gave him a hug. My brother Grant said you hugged a nigger. I looked at him and said what if it was our mother.

I didn't date or go to the movies until I was sixteen. On Saturday nights we went to a neighbor's house for square dancing. Bob Hartzburg and his wife Laura and another neighbor were our protectors if they didn't go we couldn't go. Bob was the caller it was a lot of fun. They were good people. Most always we had a good crowd.

Now to add some humor in this masterpiece. I had trouble every month with my periods. The doctor told mother to get me a bottle of Lydia Pinkhams. After taking a couple doses I put the bottle up in the cabinet thinking no one would get it. Well Grant saw it and wondered why we were hiding it. Without reading what it was he took a drink thought it was pretty tasty and he drank the rest that was in the bottle. When I asked him about it he asks me what it was for. Being mean, I told him he would find out soon enough when he started having periods every month. He would get mad at me for asking him if had his period yet. Until mother asked me to quit however, she thought it was funny too.

Back in the 1920's not very many women drove so they depended on a man who was called the peddler who came around about every two weeks. This peddler would have some staples, thread, fabric, powder, cough syrup etc. Things that most country women needed. He would take eggs, chickens and sometimes garden produce for payment. He then sold them to city women. We kids looked forward for his arrival. He sometimes had candy, mostly suckers, for a penny.

I remember one time when it was the middle of the week, Mother was looking in the cabinet to see what she could cook. She said "I am out of flour and cornmeal, I don't know what to feed you kids." I replied "how about vegetable soup, it's filling and good." I told her I would go the cellar and bring up a couple jars. But first I wanted to go get the mail. Our mail box was almost a mile down the road. We got some papers. I happened to look and there was a quarter on the ground. I swear it wasn't there before. Another angel? When I got back home I asked mother if she would like for Gail and me to town and get some bread. The grocery store where Duesterburg's drug store used to be of Sixth Street. They sold day old bread three for 25 cents. When we got there a lady told us that Opells bakery on Second Street was selling day old bread for 5 cents a loaf. That sounded good, we asked her how to get there and she told us it was a long hike. This bakery was a block from Sacred Heart Church. When we made it back home walking all the way mother scolded us. However, I think she was proud of us too. Egg sandwiches were good and toast with jelly was a perfect dessert.

Mark 10,13-16:
People were bringing little children to Jesus to have him touch them but the disciples rebuked them. When Jesus saw this, he was indignant. He said to them, "Let the little children come to me, and do not hinder them, for the kingdom of God belongs to such as these. I tell you the truth, anyone who will not receive the kingdom of God like a little child will never enter it. And he took the children in His arms, put his hands on them and blessed them.

CHAPTER 8

Move To Vincennes

IN THE FALL of 1932 mother decided we should move to town and find jobs. Put the kids in school, Paul was almost six years old. It would be his first year in school. Mother rented a house on Emison Ave for $7.00 a month. The canning factory was across the railroad tracks. It was tomato canning time so; mother, Edith and I went to work. We earned 12 cents an hour. Every morning there was a line of people wanting a job. It was seasonal work. We tried to put money back to help us pay bills during the winter. It was a rough time.

A friend of mine and his wife asks me if I would like to take care of his mother who had breast cancer. They lived south of Olney Illinois. Not knowing if I could get work or not I told him yes. It was $4.00 a week room and board. The couple had a nice home and a small country store which was always busy. There also was a one room school and a church which I attended on Sunday morning. There were really nice people in Elbow, Illinois. I kind of felt at home there the town reminded me of Beal. After the death of Mrs. Brown I moved back home. In Vincennes

I cleaned houses for fifty cents an hour and baby set for twenty five cents or if I was lucky fifty cents an hour.

There was a theater on North Second Street called Alice run by a Mr. Thorne. He showed a lot of good movies. Sometimes you could get in for ten cents; those nights he ran two features. He had big crowds mostly young people.

Then there was Gregg Park, we would visit, swing and run races. There were a lot of things going on in the park. Life bands performed regularly and medicine shows were common entertainment.

July of 1936 my heart was broken. Gail and a friend of his were working.

They were doing cleanup work at Dumes junk yard. Gail got caught in some electric wires and died instantly. Gene his friend tried to help him, he ran for help, but it was too late. I will always remember the times we worked together to help mother with food and bills. Each day I tell Gail how much I love him and how I miss him. A lot of things have happened since 1936.

Matthew 5,4:
Blessed are those who mourn, for they will be comforted.

CHAPTER 9

Respect Elders

WE KIDS WERE always taught to obey and show respect for our elders. They thought they could do everything, but when my dad wanted to build a room onto our house, no blue prints or patterns, it turned out fine. Until one night when the rain came and the room was full of water. Putting on a tin roof was a really bad mistake. Dad didn't lap the sheets over so every nail hole was leaking. We kids thought it was funny. We also felt sorry for mom and dad. Uncle Len, dad's older brother, came to the rescue. He took the tin roof off and put tar paper on and then the tin sheets, over lapping each row.

Years later Uncle Len built a house where they lived for years. I stayed with their younger kids so Aunt Dean could help him. We went with them several times, had picnic lunches. We played games. I loved Uncle Len and Aunt Dean very much; they were my favorite aunt and uncle.

I was about nine years old and I will never forget the time my Grandma Deckard was our Sunday school teacher for my age. I was reading my little card we got every week. Grandma pulled me up from my seat pulled up my dress and spanked me. Of course I ran to Mother crying because I didn't know why she did that. I had always loved her. When Mother asked her what I was doing, she said Lila wasn't doing anything wrong. The other children were acting up and didn't listen to her. I thought by spanking Lila they might think they would be next for not listening and behave better. Well little stubborn me, I wouldn't speak to Grandma for a long time. Dad told her to tell me she was sorry. Also from then on mother or he would punish me if I needed it. In other ways she was a good grandma. I love all my Grandkids. I have 9 grandkids, 20 great grandkids, 14 great great grandkids and 1 great great great grandkid. There are 6 generations in my family.

We all have favorite teachers we liked and learned more from because we connect with them more. Mine was Miss Martha; she taught health, sewing and cooking classes. She would bring me books from the library to read. Books that were clean and funny like Little Women, Girl of the Limberlost, Heidi, Huckleberry Finn.

Leviticus 19, 32:
Rise in the presence of the aged, show respect for the
elderly and revere your God. I am the Lord.

Neighbors

Staff photo by Matt Murschel

LILA WESLEY

A late bloomer, Lila Wesley keeps busy with the love of life

BY DANELLE KIEFFNER
staff writer

Some might call Vincennes resident Lila Wesley a late bloomer.

She was 55 when she learned to drive and she was in her late 60s when she opened her own business.

Now 80, she enjoys doing both in addition to spending time with her 10 grandchildren, 17 great-grandchildren and four great-great-grandchildren.

Lila playfully winces at the sound of her own words — great-great-grandchildren.

"See how old I am," she said, laughing.

Her daughters, JoAnn Lambert and Marilyn Doades shake their heads.

"She can work circles around us," JoAnn said.

Most of the Missouri native's energies are directed toward her first love — the church.

When her church, Vincennes Church of God, needed a clerk, she was there.

When the church decided to remodel awhile back, the 80-year-old was there — albeit as "The Boss," of course, she said with a smile.

This particular day, Lila entertains a bevy of guests in her quaint home on Vigo Street. Dressed to the nines, the visitors occupy every chair and every space on the living room sofa.

Unlike many of Lila's callers, these fail to partake in the conversation she loves so much. They can't — they're dolls.

Lila dressed the donated babes in adorable apparel for the church of which she is a charter member. She doesn't mind doing things for the church, especially since part of her zest for life can be attributed to her strong faith.

"The Lord keeps you going," she said.

In spite of her many years of experience on this earth, Lila continues to do just about anything she wants, including making and selling crafts, working in the store and shopping among other things. She loves being around people, a luxury her Rainbow Shoppe affords her.

"We cry together and we pray together," she said of the memorial flower shop patrons who are actually more like family to her.

Lila has never not been around people. She was one of 11 children.

When she was old enough, she worked in retail sales, her career path placing her at Ayres, Hills and the old Grants store. She eventually owned and operated a women's boutique, Mode O Day, in Vincennes.

Lila's fondest retail memories, however, are at Grants where she worked in just about every department except the restaurant.

She vividly recalls one particularly awkward incident that occurred while she was working in the shoe department.

The former salesgirl explained a man with a wooden leg had come into the store for a pair of boots. Eager to please, she slipped a boot onto his foot, a boot she soon discovered was too small. It was stuck — and good.

After tugging and tugging, the duo were unsuccessful at removing the boot. Finally, the situation forced the customer into the dressing room where he had to remove his leg in order to remove the boot. Needless to say, he didn't leave the store with a pair of boots that day, she added, laughing.

Grants was a part-time stint for Lila who spent her daylight hours at the phone company.

Today's schedule is far less hectic. Having her own shop in her own back yard has allowed the wife of the late "Doc" Wesley time to putter in her garden and also sew.

Her children JoAnn, Marilyn and Larry aren't surprised by their mother's endless abundance of energy. Their grandmother was the same way.

Marilyn said Lila's mother painted her house herself at the age of 72 and at 92 was still working in her garden in the heat of the Knox County summer.

One thing is for sure, Lila loves being involved — and busy.

"If anybody has anything to do…" Lila said.

"…she's right there in the middle of it," JoAnn added.

28

Knox County peaches

By Brian Spangle

2008

Eighty summers ago, in August 1928, orchardists in Knox County were bringing in a bumper crop of peaches. Besides good weather conditions, the main reason peaches were so plentiful that season was because there were more acres of peach trees bearing fruit. An unnamed big local grower predicted he would have a 20,000 bushel crop, and he claimed he spent more than $5,000 on peach baskets. Others were expecting in excess of 10,000 bushel crops.

Orchards, both large and small, dotted the county at that time. Those who placed newspaper ads to sell peaches that season were: John Dyer's McKenney Farm; B. F. Nesbitt; W. C. Teschner's Delicious Orchards; Simpson Orchard Co.; Carl F. Meyer; H. F. Crook; Palmyra Orchards; Curtis T. McClure; Dixie Orchard Co.; R. M. & J. T. Hogue; J. W. Kimmell Fruit Farm; O. J. Klein; and Luther Scott's Peach Orchards.

There were many other peach orchards in Knox County, notable among them being those of Newton Yates and Burt Yates.

Varieties of peaches on the market were Hiley Belle, South Haven, Elberta, and Hale, the latter two being the most common.

Peach crops in other parts of the country were also good that year, but overall the abundance of fruit was a mixed blessing for growers. There were simply too many peaches, so they did not bring high prices. In Knox County, peaches were selling for 50 cents to $2.50 per bushel.

Many peaches were sold right at the orchard sheds. The Tip Top Creamery bought them to make fresh peach ice cream. Others were trucked out or shipped by rail to out of state markets.

Besides quantity, the quality of local peaches was also excellent. One pound peaches were common and some were as big as 20 ounces.

Vincennes Sun Commercial article about the over abundance of peaches in 1928

Ruth and Vivian are cute

In their feed sack dresses.

These three guys are Grant

Gail and Loren

Me at age 38 when I worked

at Ayers in Indianapolis

My 8th grade picture

Carrie Deckard at age 95 she is holding
great-great grandson John Kellams

My daughter JoAnn with goat and buggy.

Lila at age 91 relaxing on the 4th of July.

Missouri kids: Me in front with Grant and Oma and Edith in the back. Notice the large bows in our hair.

Our cook stove had a reservoir on the end.

We always had hot water.

Pump hard to get some running water.

Flat iron was heated on the wood burning stove
It was wise to have at least 2 irons. One

heating up and one in use.

Heating stove: A pot of beans set on top

cooked all day like the slow cookers of today.

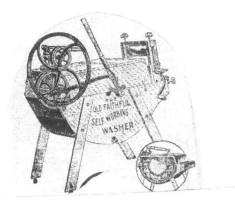

This washing machine had a wringer. Mom and I

did a lot of laundry on a machine like this one.

Mother's sewing machine served her until her death.

CHAPTER 10

Instructions

MOTHER, EDITH AND I didn't always agree on everything. For instance about the Bible. They believed Acts 2:38 is the only way to be baptized to get into heaven. But in Matthew 28:19 Jesus says to be baptized in the name of the Father, Son and Holy Ghost. Jesus will let me know some day. Anyway I pray to be with Him in heaven. I ask all of you to be at least 100 years old. Stay young like your grandma Lila. Thank God I never smoked or drink hard whiskey or beer. I cannot stand the smell of them. I do like to eat, fish is my favorite meat. I like about all the vegetables even spinach.

We all need a home church where we can be happy hear the word of God and feel like we have been to church. Instead of going to just hear the latest gossip. Sunday school is very important that's where we learn. I taught for several years to ages 6 to 10 year olds. At one time I had 25 boys and girls in my class. If any of you are ever ask to teach, do it you will be blessed.

The little church I attended about 30 years is no longer a church. It was sold for lack of attendance. The older people have passed away the younger ones married, moved away or went to their spouses church. I really miss attending church but it's a hardship. I fell and broke my right hip in 2003. I still have to use a walker and quit driving. That was hard to do. Marilyn and Leon are so good about taking me to the doctors and to pick up my medicine.

The other night I asked God why I was still here and able to remember years back so well. I am the only one left in our grade school class and in the Church I attended. Aunt Ruth and I are the only ones left in our family of eleven children.

I am so glad mother lived to see television, automatic washer, dryers and most of you kids. She once said she had the best grandkids ever. Some of you great grandkids remember her. She would really be upset by the news today. She often talked about things that are going on today. She said the Bible will be full filled wars, country divided, churches destroyed. I see it every day be careful who you trust and keep God in your hearts.

All I can do anymore is take one day at a time. I have a lot of good memories about people I worked with and customers that came into my flower shop. We called it the Rainbow Shoppe. We sold silk flowers for a bush of seven flowers for 89 cents. We also had saddles, wreaths, vases and anything needed for the cemetery. I mostly miss the people. A lot of prayers and tears were shared. I have seen a lot of men cry because of the loss of a loved one and they are buying flowers for the first time.

Chapter 11

Animals To Love

THE OLD SAYING is a dog is man's best friend. Most animals will be your friend if they are treated and fed well. When we lived in the country we had a big barn which only housed our cow, Daisy. A man by the name of Bob was working in the strip mine and needed some place to keep his horses. They were big and beautiful. He told me not to get around them or let the kids go near them. He fastened them up in stalls. I felt so sorry for them. Bob said his wife was scared to death of them. They probably knew that. Or maybe she didn't talk to them; anyway it didn't take long for me to make friends with them. I gave them carrots, apples once in a while. I peeled and seeded the apples; they looked forward to that treat.

We had a German Shepard dog by the name of Queenie. She was really smart and protective. One night she woke me up barking and scratching at the door. She was trying to tell me to go with her. I slipped on a robe and went outside she took me down to the pasture. Your grandpa was working, just me, the kids were asleep. The horses were both down there and one of them had his foot caught in the fence. I said a prayer for God to help me. I then went to the tool shed and got a crow bar. I knocked the board loose and his foot came right out. The foot was not injured in anyway. The horses followed Queenie and I back to the barn. I told Bob the next morning that he better check on his horse's foot to see if it was OK. I told him what happened he said it's a wonder they didn't kill me. "God must have been looking after you the horses and Queenie" he said. After that happened those horses became more friendly.

Our cow, Daisy was the best friend anyone could have. She not only gave us plenty of milk. butter and cottage cheese, but also was very lovable. For instance one day I was sitting on the back step shelling peas. Daisy was in the barn lot. There was a loose board in the fence next to the gate. Daisy raised it up and came up and laid her head in my lap. She rolled her big brown eyes at me, she wanted to be petted. I put her back in the lot and fixed the fence. That is after I petted her and talked to her about getting out of the barn lot. Every time I see a cow I remember Daisy.

Tomboy, a stray cat, came to the back door begging for food. He is a beautiful cat, black and white. He was so skinny I didn't know if I wanted to keep him or have him picked up. Over the weekend we all fell in love with him. He is so smart, gentle and keeps himself clean. He stays under our wood deck. I guess he is a keeper. Sometimes he strays off and we miss him. So far he always comes back for food and water. He gets in the house often looks around then wants out. Strange how we connect with animals.

When your uncle Larry lived in the country his landlord had a cornfield in the back of the house. Like a lot of 4year old boys L.D. wanted to hide from his three older sisters. The family called him and he kept running and crying. We could hear what sounded like hogs grunting and we could tell they were close. His dad told him to sit down and to answer when he called him. That worked. It didn't take long to find out where he was. Just like our heavenly Father if we sit still and answer his voice He will find us. I hear a lady say one time I found the Lord, my reply was "He wasn't lost you were He was there all the time.

By the way the noise we heard was not a herd of hogs after L.D. On the other side of the corn field was a field that motorcyclist used to race. Now we know why they call them hogs.

Genesis 1:24 &25
And God said "Let the land produce living creatures according to their kinds: livestock, creatures that move along the ground, and wild animals each according to its kind". And it was so. God made the wild animals according to their kinds, the livestock according to their kinds, and all the creatures that move along the ground according to their kinds, and God saw that it was good.

CHAPTER 12

Take Time To Listen

WE HEAR AND read a lot about small business it's not only about the money I don't believe many people get rich. It's about the friends you make and everyday lives, the family troubles and happy times we each have. A few years ago when I had my flower shop open, I'll never forget the little boy with the bluest eyes. He was about 10 years of age came in the shop, it was Mother's day. I was getting ready to leave for church. I couldn't turn him away; he wanted some flowers for his mother. He started crying and then told me his mother was mad at him and told him to go outside. Anyway he bought her a half dozen red roses. I told him if his mother didn't like the color to bring them back after dinner and exchange them. I gave him a hug and said if you were my son I would love any color. He came back that afternoon and said his mother cried when he told her what I said. She loved the roses and him. We all have our off days. That's life.

Paul, a boy about 12 years of age, who was in my Sunday school class, a real clean cut young man who lived not too far from me. He rode his bike down to the shop and looked around for a while then asks me if he could talk to me. I always find time for young people. He told me he had younger siblings and his real father left when he was about seven. The father didn't keep in touch with his mother or him. His mother remarried and he felt like his stepdad didn't like him either. After I asked him a few questions about his stepdad, I found out he had never been married or been around children. He was an only child. The advice I gave him was to make the first move. Go home and ask him to play basketball or catch with you which ever you like best. On Saturday suggest going to the river or lake and fish for a while, talk to him about sports, etc. I know you two will hit it off fine. Just let me know how things turn out. Paul came to see me before they moved to another state when the stepdad was transferred. Paul thanked me said he really loved his stepdad. I think of him often, and pray that his life is special.

A steady customer and very young wife and mother of two boys came in one afternoon crying. My first thought was something terrible has happened. I started playing with the boys until she got settled down. Then she told me that she and her husband were having problems. They had just built a new home. His work slacked down and he wanted to sell the house. She loved the house so much, it was her dream home. They could not afford the high payments. She asks me what I would do. Again I had to think a while before I said anything. "Honey, I asked her "which do you care about the most a nice expensive house or your family". She answered "my family". Later she came in and said they got enough out of the house to buy a two bedroom home in a nice neighborhood, a big yard for the boys. She was a different person. No worries I would guess. I see her once in a great while.

Back to family. I was babysitting with my granddaughters they were about three or four years old at the time. One blond, blue eyes and the other was a red head with blue eyes both were cute as buttons. The girls played together real well. I had ironing to do, remember when we ironed everything baskets full. I told the girls they could play outside if they would stay in the backyard and not to go out the gates. I finished the ironing and checked on the girls. What a mess! They had given each other a mud bath from head to toe. They were having a ball. I had to laugh remembering I had done the same thing when I was a kid, with

Grant's help. Our mother spanked us. I put the girls in the bath tub. We had to change the water three times. I put their clothes in the washer and dryer. My tee shirts were their time out cover ups for a while. Can you guess who these girls were? Jina and Susan, you are right. The water came out of the bird bath and dirt out of a flower pot.

Proverbs 19:20
Listen to advise and accept instruction,
and in the end you will be wise.

CHAPTER 13

Family

ANOTHER HEARTBREAK PAUL was fifteen when he decided he wanted to join the Army. Who signed his papers we never found out for sure? Mother asks me if I did, no way would I sign for baby brother to go to war. He was sent to Germany and when they found out he was fifteen they sent him home. We were all so happy. At age eighteen he had to reenlist and was sent to Korea. He was killed in service in 1950.

Grant was in the army in Germany and lost his right leg. He and a buddy were in a fox hole, his buddy was killed. War is so tragic for everyone. Grant's wife Erma wasn't well when he came home. She had a heart condition and passed away in 1951. She left my brother with a small son, Gary. Grant met Ann who lost her husband to cancer. Ann had one daughter and two sons. They married and had a happy life together until his death. Ann lost a son Bob with cancer.

Grant was running for sheriff of Knox County. He did not win. I was at the grocery store one day and I heard this woman talking to a man about Grant running for sheriff. She said "all we need is a one legged man in office". I walked up to her and said he lost his leg in Germany fighting for people like you and he happens to my brother". She apologized and was very nice about it. I guess she felt pretty low saying things she didn't know anything about. Ann and I become good friends. She is just like a real sister to me.

My other brother, Loren, was in the Coast Guard. After his discharge he lived with mother. He worked for Grant and sold used cars at his car lot. Loren did not marry until he was forty two years old. Then he remarried three times. He died in 1990 due to a heart condition.

The oldest child was Edith. She married Otis and they lived in Indianapolis most of their live. After Otis retired they bought a place in Freelandville where they lived until his death. Edith bought a house across the street and in the next block from me. She passed away at age ninety six. She had no children. She died October 26, 2005. She was 96 years old on October 12th.

Oma, the next born girl, married at the age of sixteen to Orval. Oma bore her husband fifteen children. They raised thirteen, ten girls and three boys. When the youngest was still in arms they loaded up and moved to Arizona. The oldest daughter, Helen, was married and she stayed in Indiana. Oma made most of the girl's clothes even wedding gowns. She also baked the wedding cakes. She had many talents.

Vivian married Vermont and she bore him four boys and then she had a little girl. After Vermont's death she married Frank who she met at work. They were both employed at Hamilton Glass.

Ruth, the baby girl, moved to Indianapolis after graduating from high school. She met Bill a plumber and they married. They had three girls and then two boys. Bill had a very good plumbing business in Lawrence, Indiana. After he retired they bought a farm near Vevay. Indiana. Bill was found out in the field by one of the sons he died of a heart attack. Ruth then married Nat and lived happily until his death. Ruth still lives in Vevay, Indiana.

Mother died on October 26, 1989. We tried to take care of her in our home, but her legs gave out on her. She couldn't help us transport herself from the wheelchair to the bed. I was in my early seventies and just too old to lift on her. She had to go to a nursing home. She lived there the last two or three years of her life. I miss her so, every now and then I think I will call mom and ask her how to do such and such. Then I realize she can't be reached by phone any more.

1Timothy 5:5
The widow who is really in need and left all alone puts her hope in God and continues night and day to pray and to ask God for help.

Chapter 14

We Got Richer Every Day

IFE GOES ON. You learn to accept it one day at a time. Ours didn't change much. Same chores, games, school, the big change was when Mr. Klein's son house burned and mother said we would move out so they could have a place to live. My cousin had an empty house down at Beal. Two rooms down and two upstairs. Just a path to the road. He plowed a couple of feet from the house. We played in the road. The only good thing we could go to church and Sunday school. I will never forget the day we kids were playing and we saw a truck coming to the house. I called for mother. I told her our angels were coming to visit. Mr. Klein asks me if I wanted to move back home. The answer was yes, yes from all of us.

We could get on the school bus at the front door instead of walking a mile out to catch the bus. Some of the kids at Beal knew mother got welfare, mostly relatives. They called us welfare kids. Their parents paid tax money to keep us. Just being mean I guess.

That's enough of the hard times. The depression was still on but we didn't notice it that much. I thought we were pretty rich. We always had plenty of food and mother made our clothes. We had a good place to live and best of all we had each other.

Our cousin Everett bought Aunt Grace a gasoline washer and brought us her old one. It was made like a washboard inside. It had a big wheel you turned to wash the clothes and a wringer. I loved doing the wash on it. I said to mother," We get richer every day." I can still hear her say "you silly girl that's still work". We didn't have to put our hands in hot water or wring the clothes by hand.

Shoes, I don't remember ever going to town to buy new shoes. Mother always measured our feet and bought the shoes a little big knowing that in a few weeks we would grow into them. I remember the shoe last used to put new soles on worn shoes. You could buy kits with leather to half-sole shoes. Shoes strings were a nickel a pair or you tied your old strings together if they broke. In 2003 the Beal church celebrated the 80th year. My son, Larry, was home visiting from Arizona. We went to the church in the afternoon to visit. To me it was like going back home. Out front of the church an electric wire held a pair of shoes. Who hung them there or how is a mystery. Was it Satan leaving or a saint called up and left them hanging? Parts of the shoe strings held them on the wire. The tongue is the evil one and the sole is the part that wears out first. The heel is one that causes you more pain. Think about this before you answer. Kids, I love the shoes that light up they are cool. Back in my day we would never dream of how things have changed.

In June 1937 I married Theodore (Doc) Wesley. I met him and his sister Amanda at Gregg Park. We worked at the same place. We went to the Justice of Peace during our lunch hour one day and got married. The marriage lasted for twenty three years. He taught me a lot. I learned how to hang wallpaper, clean wallpaper and paint. This knowledge was a big help to me later when I bought this house I live in now. I have lived here fifty six years this September 2012. Also don't trust all the people you love, you can get hurt. Doc liked to drink and chase women. Change of life so they say, enough of that.

We remained friends; he died in July 1970 at the age of fifty seven. I don't allow drinking, smoking or swearing in my home. God has blessed me with jobs when I needed them. good neighbors and a close church family. I have had two new cars, a 1972 Nova and a 1992 Shadow. I really miss my car but I fell and broke my right hip on December 9, 2003 and had to give up driving.

Mother in her later years (she died at age ninety seven) told me to keep in touch with her family. Most of them live in Missouri. She really loved her family. My dad's older brother stayed in Popular Bluff and raised his family there. We try to go to Sikeston every June for the family reunion.

I don't remember a lot about my grandma, she died pretty young. I loved Grandpa Jaynes he came up to visit us several times. He traveled by train, we would go to the depot to meet him. He loved to dance so my husband and I took him one Saturday night to the Ben Hur. That was a dance hall downtown. There was a crowd there that night. A lot of single women attended. I didn't know grandpa could dance so good. The women would tap another woman on the shoulder to dance with him. He taught them a lot of new steps. When we got back to Mothers she said Pa could always dance.

Grandpa came to visit during the World War II. My husband was working at a plant in Charlestown Indiana. Doc was only home on weekends. I got really sick, appendicitis, and had to have surgery. JoAnn was three years and Larry was nine months old. Mother was working. I was so happy to see him. He went home with me to help care for my kids. He was a special Granddad, I am sure I will see him again in heaven. He loved his family. However we are a very loving family.

This is something I must add to this book so you will know more about us as a family.

Moms try this and see if it works for you. When JoAnn, Larry and Marilyn were little I wasn't feeling very good. So we all laid down to rest I told them the first one who hears the penny drop gets a treat when we get up. They were real quiet and finally fell asleep. They all three got cookies and said Mom you tricked us. It was funny.

Another thing they finally caught on to was their Dad told them we couldn't go up town at night because they rolled up the sidewalks. They asked me how they did that I said ask your Dad it's his story. Of course that didn't last long for them to know that wasn't possible.

Another thing he told them to write to Santa and then put the letter in the stove for Santa to get it. I stopped that for fear they would get burned. I don't know how many letters Santa received. Kids today know better they have television, computers, more books and preschool.

When we lived in the country at Wheatland Larry wanted to hunt rabbits. He was way too young for a gun. His Dad told him to try the salt shaker system. If Larry could shake some salt on the rabbit's tail he could catch the rabbits. Well Larry believing everything his Dad told him runs all over the fields chasing rabbits with the salt shaker in hand. Needless to say we did not eat rabbit that night.

You kids are growing up so fast it's hard to keep up with everything you do. Harold the oldest grandchild was so cute and spoiled rotten Carrie is the oldest granddaughter and Sandra are JoAnn's children. Larry has four children; Lucinda, Angela(deceased) Carol and L.D. or Larry David. Marilyn has three children, Anita,Lee and Jina. Lee was born in Alaska I call him my little Eskimo. Among the three kids I have ten grandchildren, eighteen great grandchildren, eleven great great grandchildren and one great great great granddaughter.

I love you all and proud to call you all my family. Just take one day at a time and pray and give thanks to God. That's the way I lived to be almost ninety seven years old. You can make it!

Proverbs 17,6:
Children's children are a crown to the aged, and
parents are the pride of their children.

CHAPTER 15

Family Additions

Now that it is getting late and you all are getting ready to go home with your gifts exchange and some goodies. Don't forget your zucchini bread. I bake bread for all families and neighbors. My gift to you for Christmas. I will try to remember the best of my adult life.

A young boy named Jim had just lost his mother and he lived with his grandparents. He came over to the house and asked me if he could live with us and finish his senior year of high school. He could help in the bicycle shop. We had a two bedroom house and three children. We went out and bought another roll away bed. Larry slept in the same room with JoAnn and Marilyn. They were all young kids sharing a room didn't bother them. Jim slept in the living room. He was such a nice young man just like my own kid. Jim raked leaves and shoveled snow to make spending money. For Christmas we bought him clothes which he needed real bad. He cried and said "Thanks mom" and of course I cried too. He started dating Dorothy, a sweet girl. He got a steady job at the Goodrich store. I don't think he made big money. Dorothy cleaned houses and baby sat. When they told me they were getting married I was happy for them. I knew these kids would make it, they had one daughter. Jim was a minister at a small church on Bunker Hill for a while. Then they moved to Bloomington, Indiana. Larry and I went to see them twice. I miss their phone calls, Christmas cards etc. They are both deceased.

In the late seventies my granddaughters Carrie and Sandy attended Vincennes University and met Sauraya. She was from Kuwait. She is a beautiful girl and so smart. Sandy got married and Sauraya asked if she could move in with us. She helped with the cooking, fixed dishes that were delicious. She liked our American food also. After she spent two years here she went to Carbondale Illinois to take engineering courses. She met her husband, also an engineer. They live in Nashville Tennessee. Both are engineers for the state. They have two handsome boys. We visited them one weekend and she came to my 90th birthday. She and her youngest son came to Carrie's 50th, birthday party.

Margaret, a very sweet girl from China lived with us while attending the local University. She lived in California after completing her education at several colleges in America. She now lives near Denver Colorado and works for an investment firm. Margaret loves animals she has two cats and two dogs. Plus she has a horse that she enters in contest for jumping, etc. She has a wall full of ribbons that she has earned riding this horse. JoAnn and Carrie went to Margaret's to visit for a week and had a great time seeing sites in the mountains. Carrie took Sandra's two kids, John and Mary for a visit one time also. Margaret comes home for Thanksgiving and cooks the dinner for us. I love Chinese food, but she cooks turkey for the main part. You have to meet her to love her. As Nancy says "You got to read it to know what's in it".

Rhonda, a third cousin to me spent most of her younger life in an orphan's home or foster homes. Her mother wasn't able to care for her, the younger sister and brother. I picked up the girls and took them to Sunday school with me. A lady at Decker took Timmy with her. I am not sure if she adopted him or not. He is a grown man now. Rhonda's case worker called me to see if Rhonda could live with me. She said they would pay me $150.00 a month. They paid all of her medical bills. She didn't have any clothes that fit her or looked fit to wear to school her senior year. So we went shopping for underwear and shoes. Back then in 1976 you could buy a lot of clothes for 150.00 dollars. We bought material and made dresses, skirts, slacks and vest. She had a lot of mix and match outfits. I wanted her to have as nice clothes as Carrie and Sandra had. They all three were dressed to be proud. They all worked week ends but at different places. Carrie and Sandra worked at the Waffle House. Rhonda worked at Charlie's different hours a lot of the time. Carrie had a car, no problem there. They had to buy their gas and pay for the insurance. We found a good used car for Rhonda after she finished driving lessons. On her 18th birthday she didn't want to follow our rules. The girls were to be home after their shifts were over or at least call. But one night Rhonda didn't come home or call. She said she slept in her car all night. I was so worried about her I couldn't sleep. I had to be at work at 6:00 a.m. I guess I was a little cross with her and I am sorry about that. Anyway she said this couple wanted her to stay with them. She moved out, she wasn't happy there either. She went to Evansville to take care of a lady and lived in with her for several years. She is married to a nice guy named Greg. They come up often now to see me and she calls me. She told me she was sorry she left. When kids turn eighteen or before they don't want to listen to anyone. Later after they grow up they realize their foolishness. I love you Rhonda.

As of now the last count I have nine grandchildren. Plus Angela Wesley who passed away on December 27, 1999. She died of cancer and lupus at age thirty six. We were told when she was twelve that she had lupus. She did not have a very active life. We all miss her. I have sixteen great grandchildren, fourteen great great grandchildren and one great great great granddaughter. Yes we have six generations. Marilyn took a picture of the six generations to the newspaper office for publication. They didn't print it for several days, when we inquired why it hadn't been printed. We were told they didn't believe it was true. They had never had six generations before.

I am so proud of my off springs. The spouses are welcome also to my family.

Matthew 18:5
And whoever welcomes a little child like this in
my name welcomes me. (Jesus quotation.)

CHAPTER 16

After Thoughts

ARE WE BETTER off today than we were 4 years ago? Ask the people who lost their jobs. Our September 5th newspaper ran two and one half pages (small print) of home and business up for sheriff sales for back taxes. There was a total of 508 pieces of property on that list. As you know if you are not working you can't pay income taxes or property tax.

I am so thankful for President Franklin Roosevelt coming up with the idea of Social Security. It is like a pension or savings for us as we get older. We all paid into Medicare for years while we worked. The power people today is spending it for whatever they want, You kids fight for things to change this procedure or you may be taking care of your parents or any older person you know. Just take care of each other, love thy neighbor.

In 1962 I owed $11.00 in income taxes. The tax collector came in the store where I worked. He talked real mean and loud to me about garnishing my wages if I didn't pay them by the next day. Back then I brought home $70.00 every two weeks. I really forgot about it until I paid my home taxes. God takes care of us. I was off work the following day until 11:00 o'clock. My mail carrier came about 10:00 o'clock and again I had an angel. In the mail was a check for $11.00 from the light company for my deposit. I cried and thanked the good Lord. I stopped at the court house and paid my debt to Leo, a real nice man. I had worked with him years before. His wife and I were good friends. Anyway there were so many complaints against the collector that he got fired. Don't let a job take over your life.

I hear on the news today a lot of people owe thousands of dollars in taxes. You know they are our leaders in our capital of D.C. Let me know how you public servants get by with not paying taxes. A lot of us working people would like to know. I want an answer from you before Election Day.

I never dreamed I would live to see television, cell phones, computers, instant meals nor a microwave to heat them in. Washers and dryers that you just push buttons to do the laundry. Throw away diapers, dishwashers, and self-clean ovens. You kids today are really rich as mother would say if she was still with us. Like taking clothes out of the dryer ready to wear. No ironing which took a lot of time in my younger days.

When we girls got together for coffee the subject of fashion came up one morning. We all agreed Jackie was the best dressed for a first lady. The pill box hats were really popular in fact I bought several at that time. But today you don't wear hats to church or funerals. In fact I wear scarfs and rain bonnets. Barbara was really special mother type or the next door neighbor. One you could borrow a cup of sugar or exchange cookies. I have her recipe for chocolate chip cookies from her book. I always wanted to meet her, maybe someday. Then Laura would fit in with all of us. She is so down to earth and funny I have her books and will read them again someday. She is a special person also.

Now back to the doll story Dad made me give away the only doll I ever had. Well as of today I have over one hundred dolls. They include Mother Teresa, Lucille Ball, Ronald Regan, George W. Bush Raggedy Ann and Andy etc. They will be divided among the great grandkids after I am gone. My granddaughter Carrie and I were shopping one day. I was looking at dolls and told her the story about my first doll. After that she and the other kids and friends started giving me dolls for my birthday,

Mother's day, and Christmas. I bought one at a family reunion auction in Sikeston MO. I thank you all, you have made my days.

There is one of many miracles in my life that I must tell you about. I was working as the matron at the telephone company. My neck became stiff and very painful. So painful that Carrie went to work with me. She did the heavy work and mopped the floors. I could not turn my head in either direction. The next day was Sunday. The church's congregation prayed for me at both the morning and evening services. No help. After I went to bed I was talking to the Lord and was telling Him about my problem. Suddenly a man was standing beside my bed. I got up and checked the doors. They were both locked. I realized my neck pain was gone and I could turn my head. I called my daughter JoAnn and told her what had happened. Her reply was "I will be right over". She and I shouted and danced all over this house praising the Lord for healing me in an instant.

In June 1939 a man came to town with a cart pulled by a goat. He was taking pictures of kids sitting in the cart. He charged $2.00. The man told me a lot pictures were taken that day. JoAnn was sixteen months; see her picture in the family album section of this book.

Matthew 14:35 & 36
And when the men of that place recognized Jesus they sent
word to all the surrounding country. People brought all their
sick to Him and begged Him to let the sick just touch the
edge of His cloak, and all who touched Him were healed.

Epiloque

By JoAnn Lambert, Lila's daughter

I remember when…we lived on Jefferson Street in Vincennes. I must have been about four years old. My younger brother Larry was a toddler. He is two and one half years younger than me. He was still in diapers and on occasion would mess them. I can still see him coming thru the back door and announcing the mishap to our mommy. I remember the morning I woke up and discovered I had a baby sister. Larry did not like the idea of a new baby in the family. He found a piece of a limb somewhere and brought it in the house to knock that thing in the head. Marilyn the baby was so small her first crib was a shoe box. She weighed four pounds.

I loved living on Jefferson Street. We were a block from Kimmel Park. In those days the park was beautiful. Dogwood trees lined the drive through the park. A reflection pool was in front of the shelter house. Gold fish and tadpoles flourished in the pool. The shelter house was used for a dance hall sometimes during the summer. There are several picnic areas in the park. They are built of stones and contain outdoor grills. What fun we had eating lunch or a snack in one of these picnic areas. Every Fourth of July a carnival set up in the park. Fireworks were the final thrill for the holiday. We always had a houseful of company for the day. My dad enjoyed the holiday so much he built a garage in our back yard to view the fireworks from the roof. It was ironic that we had his funeral on the Fourth of July in 1970.

The house was small, four rooms and a path. We had city water, a faucet in the front yard. In the back yard between the toilet and the house was a cherry tree. One time a swarm of bees took a liking to the tree. We could not get to the toilet for fear of being stung, so we had to use the pot until a man came and gathered up the bees. We had a lot fun playing games with the neighborhood kids. We had a large vacant lot next to the house. Dad always planted a garden in the rear of the lot. The front half was a baseball diamond or a cowboys and Indians shoot-um-up area. Every kid in the neighborhood had a gun and holster and a broomstick horse. We always had bikes, scooters and tricycles. Dad had a bicycle repair shop in the garage.

During the years we lived on Jefferson Street my dad worked at an ammunition factory and got lead poisoning. His feet were so infected he could hardly walk. Mom went to work and dad became our caregiver. One morning he made oatmeal for our breakfast. Not knowing much about cooking a cereal, he cooked the entire box. Three little kids and a sick man could not eat that much oatmeal. He decided to make cookies. We had everything but raisins. We had to have raisins, so we headed out for the store. Dad could not make it walking with crutches. About halfway to the store he gave me the money to buy a box of raisins. I went on the store and made the purchase. How grown up I felt.

My parents owned the White Kitchen restaurant on Sixth Street about this time. They had built up a nice business. World War II was in progress and dad was drafted. There was no way mom could care for 3 kids and run the restaurant too so they sold it for $150.00. The war ended, dad didn't have to go after all. They tried to buy the restaurant back but the new owners would not sell. Shortly afterward they had a small restaurant on Second Street. They named it the Sugar Bowl. It was across the street from Nardines laundry and dry cleaners. On the corner was a branch of the

Knox County library. I spent a lot of time there. Some man wanted to buy the restaurant. Dad wouldn't sell. One night he came home beat up pretty bad. They used brass knuckles on him. He sold out soon after that.

When I was ten years old the house on Jefferson Street was sold. We moved to an apartment on Second Street downtown. This building was behind the Gimble Bond building. It was between Kopp's shoe store and the Liberty meat market. Now it is a parking lot for the bank. My parents opened the second Sugar Bowl on the street level and we lived upstairs.

I attended Clark Grade School which was located in the administration building at the time in 1948 or 1949. Back then every grade school put on a program on May Day. My class did a butterfly dance. Large sheets of crepe paper were fan folded. One end was pinned to our waist and the other end attached to our wrist. We pranced around the auditorium flapping our arms to expand our paper wings. Many wings tore or came loose during the program. Oh what a flop we were. The two May Day programs I remember at Tecumseh was the may pole dance and another year that we wore old clothes and our faces were blacked. I remember this one because I was chosen to lead the class in the procession.

The second Sugar Bowl did not succeed, I don't know what happened. After closing we moved to a farm near Bicknell. What a place it was. The large farm house was two stories. The down stairs was so large we didn't need the upstairs. Mom used the upstairs to dry laundry in the winter. A large red barn with a silo housed our milk cows. Also in the barn were two very large horses. They were like the horses that pull the wagon for that beer company. These horses were work horses for the nearby strip mine. Also on the farm was an equipment building. Tractors and trucks were parked there when not in use. Closer to the house was a long building. One end housed the electric pump for the water well. The other end was maybe a smoke house. We never did figure out the purpose for the built ins. On the other side of the house was a chicken house and pig sty. Dad made $27.00 a week if it didn't rain and he worked every day. We were furnished a cow for milk, a hog to butcher and chickens.

In front of the house was a large garden. Mom canned everything she could reap from that garden. The cellar was loaded with quart jars full of vegetables. It was during the family's time on the farm that I learned to sew. I made skirts and simple blouses out of feed sacks material. I was eleven years old and growing like a weed. I won two blue ribbons for sewing at the Knox County 4H fair that year. This new skill has come in handy during my adult life.

After living on the farm for a short time, dad quit that job and started working for mom's cousin Sylvan at the Palm Café. We moved to Wheatland. This house was owned by another cousin, Bob. The house was not bad, but the location was awful. The house set in the middle of fields planted with corn and wheat. You know what kind of animals live in crop fields, mice. Every time we opened a drawer mice jumped out. Mice climbed the screens on the windows. Mice were everywhere. During the short time we lived here mom got real sick with pneumonia. Dad had not come home for several days. We had no phone, no transportation, no money and absolutely no food or medicine. I had to stay home from school to care for mom and keep a fire going in the stoves. Larry and Marilyn got their lunch at school so they were doing all right. My dad's sister and her husband came to visit. They saw our condition and went to the store and bought groceries and medicine for mom.

At this time dad's problems started. Or I was old enough to realize what was going on. When I went back to school a friend asked me to go home with her for lunch. She showed me the new bikes she and her siblings got for Christmas. Their Santa was my dad. She also told me that dad stayed days at their house. The mystery of dad's absence was explained. This was the first of many times school mates told me of my dad's indiscretions. Dad started drinking heavy also, adding another big problem for our family life.

The family moved into Vincennes. We lived in three rooms of a house on 10th Street. We shared a bath room with the owners. From 10th Street to 7th Street, again three rooms and a shared bath. A two story house on 5th.

Street was our next home. Probably the best house we ever lived in. Four bedrooms and bath upstairs. The first floor had a living room, dining room and the kitchen with a pantry. The basement was clean and dry and to our delight it had a stocker furnace. This furnace had a large box connected to it. Every day we had to fill this box with small pieces of coal therefore stocking the furnace. Dad bought our first television when we lived here. After school the living room floor was full of neighborhood kid's bodies watching television.

The next move was Manila Street, the block that Rally's is on. I was in high school now. Marilyn and Larry were still in grade school. I had to go home every day and fix their lunch. By the time I walked home and fixed lunch (no time to eat) and walked back to school I was late for my typing class. The teacher would always yell at me for being late. After I explained my tardiness she was a little more tolerate. Mom's sister, Oma lived on the side of the street we did. Dad's sister Ethel lived across the street from her where the real estate office is now.

When I was fifteen years of age we lived on 15th Street. Dad had gone to Greenwood to work for an old friend Jim. Dad always did construction and home decorating. He could find work anywhere. On my sixteenth birthday, my last day at Lincoln High, we moved to Greenwood. We lived in a remodeled barn. Mom and I worked at a restaurant in Greenwood. Dad carried on with his bad habits. By this time he was a full-fledged alcoholic.

After I graduated from Center Grove High School in May of 1955 I went to work in Indianapolis as a secretary for a manufacturing company. I was only seventeen years old and not experienced for the job. My next job was at the telephone company in downtown Indianapolis. I worked as a repair dispatcher. I met a repair man named Harold and we fell for each other at first sight. We married five weeks later on April 7, 1956.

Mom got a job during Christmas at L.S. Ayers in Indianapolis. She changed into a different woman. She wore heals and makeup and dressed nicer. She says the managers at Ayers gave her self-confidence she never had before.

Mom and Marilyn moved back to Vincennes in September 1956. They moved into the house that mom and I live in now. Dad and Larry stayed in Greenwood for a while then followed mom to Vincennes. Larry graduated from Lincoln and enlisted in the Marines shortly after. Mom worked many jobs mostly two jobs at a time. She worked in dress shops, restaurants, department stores and the phone company.

Mom was fifty five years old when she learned to drive. She bought a new 1972 Nova and drove it for twenty years. My grandson now drives it he loves it almost as much as mom did. I don't ever remember a time in my live when mom did not work out of the home except for the time we lived at Bicknell and Wheatland.

The title of this book "No time for Poverty" is truly the story of her life. She has worked all her childhood and adult life. She had no time to be poor or to even consider the fact that she was living in poverty. Dad made decent money when he wasn't on a binge and could work. However, he spent it on drinks and women.

Now we have a nice comfortable poor-man's home. We have all the modern conveyances available. We can pay our bills, never worrying about the utilities being shut off. We are not rich we live from payday to payday just like most Americans do.

God has blessed these two women.

This book is a letter to Lila's Grandchildren. The next
page is a list of the names of the grandchildren. Put this
at the beginning of the book as the dedication.

Letter to my Grandchildren and Great Grandchildren

Harold Lambert

Joshua Lambert

Xander Lambert

Braydon Lambert

Tyler Lambert

Susan Lambert

Paige Lambert

Makyla Lambert

Trevor Lambert

Madison Lambert

Carrie Lambert-Fort

Sandra Lambert-Kellams

John C. Kellams

Mary E. Kellams

Lucinda Wesley Jahn

Anita Doades Morgan

Heather Wilson-Wilson

Emma Wilson

Isaac Wilson

Bennett Wilson

Melissa Wilson Carie

Nolan Carie

Liam Carie

Corbin Lee Doades

Corbin M. Doades

Corbin Ray Doades

Jaycee Doades

Christopher Doades

Adalyn Doades

Charles W. Doades

Cassandra Jahn

Lauren Jahn

Carol Wesley-Bryner

Yvonne Munch

Michael Munch

Greg Munch

David Munch

Larry David Wesley

Zachrey Wesley

Angela Wesley (died 12/28/1999)

Jina Doades-Kite

Alison Kite

Hannah Kite

Love you all Grandma Lila